The
SHORT
and
SAVVY
Guide

The Great Brain Remodel of Adolescence

How Contractors & Alligators Empower Understanding Ages 12-24

Stephanie D. Smith

ISBN: 979-8-9913807-4-4 (Paperback)

Cover Photos Attribution:
AdobeStock/Sergey Nivens (Brain)
AdobeStock/Uladzimir (Blueprint)
Alligator: Stephanie D. Smith
Cover Design and Interior Formatting: Key 3 Press
Interior Illustration: iStockphoto/jambojam (Brain)
Quote by Ronald Rolheiser (chapter 7) from *Sacred Fire: A Vision for a Deeper Human and Christian Maturity* used by permission from the publisher, Penguin Random House.

Published by Key 3 Press
https://www.key3press.com
Email: info@key3press.com

What's a "Short & Savvy Guide?"

It's a book written in a succint (but never boring) style to empower you with meaningful information you can use. Think "Just the facts, Ma'am," from the old *Dragnet* TV show. Only without the deep voice and somber face.

Reading is like dining out. Sometimes we want a place where we can linger over the menu, eat slowly, and take time deciding on dessert. Others times we opt for utensils-optional drive-throughs. This book is a blend of both. It's rich content that will deeply nourish your relationships with adolescents, but delivered in as little packaging as needed and served with a smile.

However, don't equate short with shallow. This content is more like chewing on a cut of prime rib than nibbling a marshmallow. Read thoroughly or you may miss that one point that could make a major difference!

Table of Contents

Part 1

Part 2

Part 3

What To Expect

Each section has five parts to help you not only read this book but return to it as a reference again and again!

Chapter Narrative

Core material in a traditional form.

Key Points & Tips

Bonus information, plus a selection of chapter highlights.

Worth Exploring

Suggested resources, application ideas, and mindset insights to consider for yourself and/or your adolescent.

Take Action

Practical tools to move from the information-gathering stage to the information-applying phase.

Personal Application & Reflection

Space to write your insights and ideas for your specific needs and situation. Forget what your fifth grade teacher admonished. It's okay to write in books -- at least this one!

If You're an Adolescent

I encourage you to read this book! While it's primarily written to parents, educators, and other adults, it's about you. Specifically, about your brain. (No matter what anyone has said, you do have one!) It's a very fascinating one, too!

Learning about our design -- physically, emotionally, mentally, and spiritually -- is one of the most worthwhile (and arduous) journeys we can undertake. It's not a one-time trip; personal growth is a life-long expedition only the courageous commit to.

Educate yourself about the astounding physical remodel your brain is (or will) undergo! Then have the bravery and humility to make choices which use this process to set yourself up for long-term success -- spiritually, emotionally, mentally, and relationally. You'll never regret it!

Hang On Parents!

Lucky you! You have (or soon will have) an adolescent. Are your palms sweating? Is your heart racing? Is your prayer life in or approaching "panic" mode? I get it!

As the mother of five (adult) sons, I've known the fear, frustration, joy, and delight that accompanies this transformative life season. One day you're bursting with pride, proclaiming "My kid is amazing!" The next you're burying your face in your hands, lamenting, "What did I do wrong?" Or "What's wrong with that kid?" Or both.

Parenting an adolescent can be like traversing a Class 5 river where you're just trying to avoid the submerged trees, jagged boulders, and diabolical rapids. But it can also be like floating a gentle Class 1 stream, finding refreshment in the cool water and delight in the magical landscapes. What makes a difference? Several factors, but a key one is the guide.

I want you, as an adolescent's "guide," to be equipped with confidence, effectiveness, and empathy.

My faith influences everything I write. In a few places, there's a direct reference to inviting our faith into how we guide our adolescents. If you share my beliefs, you'll be delighted. If you don't, skip over these short sections or become curious!

Grab your paddle. Don your life jacket. Pack a dry bag. (Oh, and get ready to switch metaphors.) You've got this!

Cheering for you,

Stephanie Smith

Prefrontal Cortex

Decision making
Personality expression
Social cognition
Reasoning
Values & ethics

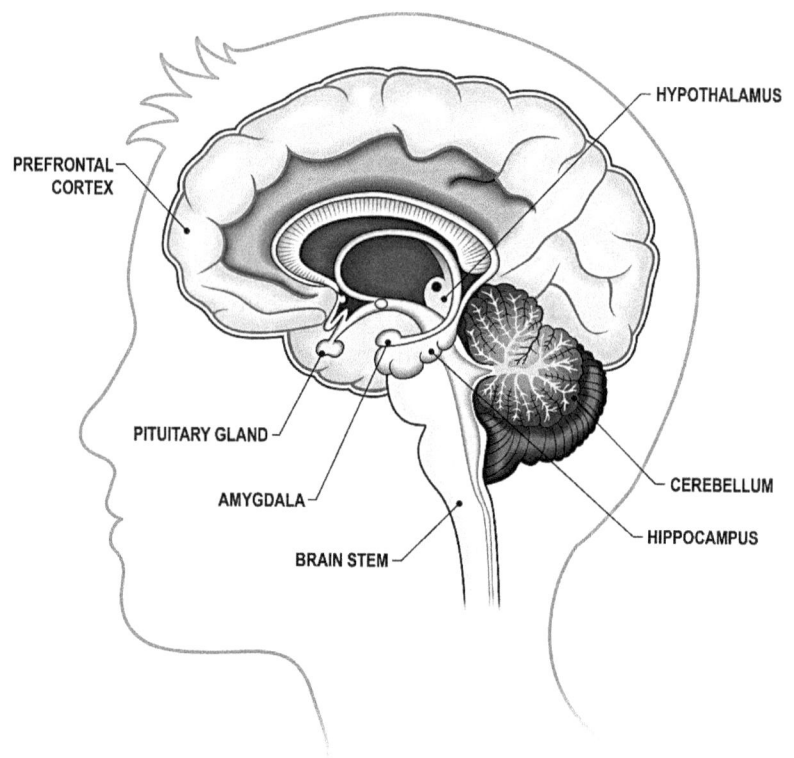

Limbic System

Emotion
Long-term memory
Behavior
Motivation
Smell

Chapter 1

What You Don't Know Can't Help (or Haunt) You

Have you ever looked at someone between the ages of 12-24 and asked yourself, "What were they thinking?" It is a rational question because (get ready to be shocked!) adolescents' brains operate differently than those of children or adults. After recovering from this profound statement, you may say, "I know what happens to the brain during adolescence. It disappears! Shuts down! Goes off-line! Hibernates!" Well, not exactly.

We hear about the "crazy hormones" of adolescence but often fail to understand their full impact on how a person thinks, perceives, and interprets the world. There is a complex and astounding renovation process which forever changes a person's physical brain and ways of thinking.

When you understand the brain remodel process, you will be more confident, effective, and empathetic.

When we lack understanding in a matter, we tend to either be arrogant or insecure. Or maybe that's just me. You're going to be empowered with scientific, research-backed data that will help you move from a place of "I don't know what's going on with this kid" to a position of, "Ah, okay, this is a normal part of adolescence, and I don't need to freak out." You will gain knowledge that will equip you to make informed decisions rather than relying on desperate, "I hope this works!" techniques. You will become more confident in raising or educating adolescents.

You will also be more effective because you can align your parenting or teaching methods with what's happening in the adolescent brain. To be effective, you must engage people in this season differently than younger children or adults.

If we're honest, (which I assume you are), we just want our familiar way of doing things to work. That's not the same thing as deciding, "I am willing to adapt my methods in order to be effective." But being the awesome person you are who is more committed to effectiveness than maintaining the status quo or following along with your peers, this book will give you tools for success. Yes, you still have to pick them up and use them appropriately, but this knowledge can be as big of a difference between cutting a 2x4 with a power saw or a hacksaw.

Third, your empathy will multiply. Have you ever had an encounter with someone and came away saying, "Wow. That person was one grumpy Gus!" Or "They're selfish!" Then you learned they'd just gone through a crushing event, and you felt like the selfish jerk? Am I the only one raising my hand?

What changed our conclusions about that person's character or social skills or personality was that we acquired new information.

We modify our expectations based on information.
Our expectations are linked to our understanding.

This book is not merely a collection of Wikipedia articles and front page Internet search engine results. I've been studying "what makes people tick" since high school. While I'm not a licensed psychologist, therapist, or psychiatrist, I am committed to a pursuit of excellence and credibility in my research.

Lest you think I write only as someone who has studied this "species" from afar, let me clear that up. I have personally taught, mentored, or engaged significantly with hundreds of adolescents. First, as a mom of five sons who were all in the adolescent stage for five straight years. For a dozen years I had at least one kid in this life stage. I came out okay -- as long as you ignore the ingrained response of checking the bathroom after guests to make sure they flushed. My sons are now safely on the other side of adolescence, but lest you think they were all beautifully behaved, let me clear that up.

At my second son's wedding his best man stood and gave an emotional toast, regaling us with years of shared life experiences. He left one out. But my oldest son decided this was a safe time to share about an outing that the three of them had during high school. I'd never heard this tale before. It involved a water tower not far from our home.

One evening this trio had the brilliant idea they should all climb to the top of our small town's water tower. Not only is this incredibly dangerous, it is also criminal trespassing. And this particular water tower was surrounded by houses in a residential neighborhood. It was also just across the highway from the police department. If someone called the police and reported this crime, the three conspirators would not have had time to (safely) descend the tower and clear the site before law enforcement arrived on the scene.

Fate was kind because no one saw or at least reported the crime in process. Or perhaps they did, but law enforcement concluded anyone dumb enough to engage in this activity deserved whatever came of it. I never inquired if this was the case. Best to leave some things in the "mystery" box.

Once they arrived at the top, Son #2 (in order of birth, not favor) had the brilliant idea it would be fun to swing back and forth – with one hand. There are certainly guardian angels who are waiting to have a word with my offspring!

I know from firsthand experience the challenges of parenting adolescents. There were other difficulties I faced which made water tower swinging escapades seem easy. But for now, if you are parenting, mentoring, or teaching an adolescent in far less than ideal circumstances, don't lose hope!

This book is not a list of formulas that guarantee everything will turn out fine if you follow them. It is powerful information plus proven principles that will increase the possibility of success.

In addition to raising five sons, I've also taught, mentored, and directed hundreds of students in various capacities. These include teaching at a private Christian school, directing a theater program, participating in speech and debate clubs, and teaching in a home education cooperative. This book is a combination of serious research and personal experience.

In the section "For Further Reading," I've listed several resources cited or referenced. In addition to these resources, I've culled from numerous articles and other books. As in most scientific fields, findings and interpretations vary between authors and researchers. Therefore, I've pulled together data that shows up consistently and have sought to avoid outliers.

Suggesting or referencing a resource does not mean I agree with all of the author's premises, findings, or applications. In scientific research and publishing, an evolutionary/no God/ no Intelligent Designer mindset dominates. It's nearly impossible in the social sciences to find research-based materials which are grounded in Biblical Christianity. It's reasonable for you to ask, "Why study findings about human design from people who don't even believe in a Designer?" The short answer is:

God is generous and gracious with distributing knowledge. He doesn't require someone to believe in him or love him before he gives capacities, desires, and opportunities for learning and understanding.

As a Christian, I find it fascinating how the very same premises or conclusions which a person attributes to evolutionary processes can fit perfectly with the Biblical view of humanity's origin and condition. Some sources have conclusions and sharp differences in application which stand clearly opposed to Christianity. We want to avoid the two extremes of "throwing the baby out with the bathwater" and "swallowing something hook, line, and sinker."

There is a possible downside to reading this book. One of the cons of being a life-long learner is "What you don't learn can't haunt you."

Have you ever said, "Oh, I wish I'd know. It would have made such a difference!" I have! Which is one of the reasons I've written this book.

New technology which gave us a window into brain development and functioning – the fMRI (Functional magnetic resonance imaging) only began to be employed in the early 2000's. My oldest son was already an adolescent. I didn't have this information available then. As I began to read findings from research, I struggled with regret and guilt as a parent. And as a teacher, I've sometimes felt I should send an apology to former students. "I'm sorry! There's so much I didn't know then!"

Don't waste today's time and energy lamenting about past practices and decisions.

We can only live from the knowledge we have, and that's why I'm so excited you're holding this book! I know you can become more confident, effective, and empathetic.

Key Points & Tips

◊ Hormones which change the body during adolescence also change the brain. This has a significant impact on how an adolescent sees and interprets the world.

◊ Desires depend on the cooperation of someone else. Goals are what you control. Memorize this truth. You're going to need frequent reminders.

◊ The more you understand about what's normal development, the less you'll take conflict or your child's poor decisions personally. Be alert to make the distinction between what's a character issue and what's physiological.

◊ Don't expect parenting techniques that worked during childhood to be effective during adolescence. You wouldn't want a surgeon to operate on your back because they were skilled with noses!

◊ Your perspective will change based on information. We modify our expectations based on what others have experienced in the past or are currently going through. Expectations connect us to understanding.

◊ Kids aren't equations to be solved. There are no formulas. They're people to be understood, guided, and loved.

◊ If you have an older adolescent or adult child, don't allow new information to become your nemesis, berating you with guilt and regret. Instead, make it your guide, informing how to repair any mistakes and make better choices now.

HOLD ONTO HOPE, NO MATTER WHAT!

◊ You may lose heart at times, but hold onto hope. Adolescents can do dumb things (think "water tower"), but their story isn't over until their last breath.

Remember, God's first two "kids" (Adam and Eve) didn't struggle with a rebellious nature and lived in a world in its perfect design. They still chose to disregard God's advice -- and he was the Perfect Parent. Take responsibility for your decisions, but don't take too much credit for your kids -- for "good" or "bad." Only God knows the whole story about why people turn out the way they do.

Worth Exploring

For a deeply moving book which demonstrates, poignantly and soberly, the power of human choice, check out Victor Frankl's timeless classic, ***Man's Search for Meaning.*** You may decide it would be a great read for your adolescent.

Need some help motivating them with "extra" reading? Don't think of cash or a pass on chores for a week or a special privilege as a bribe. Think of it the same way airlines, grocery stores, clothing boutiques, and gas stations give you rewards for purchasing from them instead of a competitor. It's savvy marketing!

Success is never achieved with good intentions; only great intentionality.

Take Action

Set aside a time to write down the desires and expectations you have for your adolescent. This may be a lengthy one-time session or it may be jotting down notes over a period of days and then organizing and polishing them.

Think immediate, short-term, and long-term. You parent out of your expectations and desires anyway. Writing them down brings them into the light. You may see you're asking too much or too little in an area. You may discover there are other areas you've never clarified for yourself or communicated to your child.

There are no guaranteed outcomes in any situation or relationship, but you can stack the odds in your child's favor with clear expectations and defined desires.

As it's appropriate, invite them to write down their expectations of themselves and (if you're really brave) of you! They may just see their expectations -- of themselves or others -- need a re-do!

Personal Application & Reflection

Chapter 2

Adolescence: Dandification or Dreadification?

Are you a home remodeling show fan? Do you love watching a designer and contractor walk into worn out places as they share a vision about what the place could be? The homeowners make their selection, and the audience is invited into the renovation process. We get to see the place transform and watch the delight of the owners as they see, for the very first time, the finished project.

I enjoy these shows; however, because I'm experienced with home renovations, I know this: It is a lot messier than it ever looks on TV. You sometimes have months of labor spliced into 30-60 minutes of footage, and no one ever goes home covered from head to toe in drywall joint compound dust. While those shows have their shortcomings, they do make a great analogy for what happens during adolescence.

As your child or student goes through this life stage, your role is going to be that of a project manager.

Your job is to maintain the vision of what can be, to

communicate with clarity to the contractors, and provide the resources and guidance for the crew to do their job.

In every house remodel, something unexpected is going to occur, and you'll have to redirect. The wall you want to remove turns out to not only be load-bearing but is filled with HVAC ducts and the main drain line. Similarly, in parenting you will encounter the unexpected. It may be a short-term phase of an attitude you never thought you'd be dealing with, or it may be an extended time of traumas and devastation that will rock your world. This is where you can maintain a vision of what can be through the power of the Holy Spirit.

One key difference is no one "chooses" to go through adolescence. People may not always know what they're getting into when they remodel, but they are making a choice to engage in that activity.

Life sends us on a journey through stages we don't control. We don't get to opt out of the challenges of toddler-hood, adolescence, middle age, or old age. We only get to decide *how* we're going to navigate those seasons, not *whether* we're going to.

Deciding how we'll maneuver life requires developing decision-making skills. Our innate knowledge is limited, and learning how to make good life choices leaves us in a place of vulnerability and dependency on others. We don't just "know" anything. We learn everything.

It can be easy to want adolescents to "just grow up," which

means, move out of this life season. We can never just decide our way out of any of life's seasons. While the physiological changes of adolescence should never excuse poor choices or behavior, it should be cause for us as parents and educators to maintain a mindset of confidence, a commitment to effectiveness, and a heart of empathy.

Adolescence is a hard season! I've heard plenty of folks say, "I wish I could go back and make some different decisions," but not, "I wish I could go back and experience those struggles all over again." The reality is it marks a stage of "no return." After adolescence, there's no going back to the naivety of childhood. No seeing the world in terms of "good guys and bad guys." There's no escaping dealing with one's sexuality. There's a recognition that, "When I grow up, I'm going to do _____" isn't going to be as easy or simple or even possible as one could think at age eight.

Grief accompanies all loss. And while it would be wrong to paint childhood as nothing but carefree days of ease and innocence, it's true there's a longing within each of us to return to a season when we didn't have a full understanding of good and evil.

We were never designed to bear the weight of evil, so the longing for "simpler times" isn't just an ache for less responsibility, but a spiritual hunger to return to the "Garden" where we knew nothing of sin.

The difficulties don't mean adolescence is only a series of painful awakenings. The same realizations which create opportunities for disappointment in oneself and disillusionment in others open up capacities for greater pleasure and purpose.

We don't want to treat adolescence like a disease to "get through." When younger children hear adults consistently refer to the "teenage" years with a sense of dread, it can provoke two reactions. The first is fear. "Will I turn into a monster?" "Will I be able to think about anything other than sex?" "Will I be able to handle the 'peer pressure' and say no to bad things?" We set children up for failure by instilling a fearful mindset about adolescence when we continue to portray this life season in such negative ways.

The second reaction is excitement. "If something called 'hormones' take over my mind and body, that sounds cool, and I can't really be held responsible for too much of what I do. Mom and Dad and my pesky sister will just have to get used to my being difficult and hard to get along with." For these children, we set them up for failure by fostering a helpless mindset. "I'm just at the whims of whatever my body feels." And we see some of this mindset today taken to extremes in regard to gender and sexuality.

The way we combat these destructive mindsets is by instilling one of empowerment. How do we do this?

First, we avoid glorifying adolescence as the "best days of your life" or an unavoidable season of horror. Rather, we want to embrace it as one of several normal life seasons which has its own unique challenges and joys.

We must avoid the two extremes of "dandification" – everything's fine and dandy – or "dreadification" – where terrors are lurking around every corner.

(I know "dreadification" is not a real world, and I'm not using "dandification" accurately. It's okay; it's one of the privileges of being a writer.)

Second, it's important to foster an attitude of confidence in your abilities to guide your child or student through this season. As it's said in football, "the best defense is a good offense." You cannot expect your adolescent to carry on with an attitude of resourcefulness and capability and strength – an empowerment mindset – if you don't live this yourself.

I know that firsthand, not because of success, but because of failure. One of my greatest parenting mistakes was being way too motivated by fear. And I didn't even recognize many motivations as being fear-based. Because I've seen the cost of that, I want to help others not make that same mistake.

See yourself as a competent (not arrogant) ship captain who knows and announces there are rough seas ahead but you are going to give the crew the training, resources, and leadership they need to get through the storms. Too often we become so fearful the crew will mutiny, we either determine we're going to run such a "tight ship" everyone will be afraid of stepping out of line or we try to please and placate everyone into cooperation.

Often in families one parent takes the "tight ship" approach and the other adopts a "let's just keep them happy" method, and the kid is left dealing with rough waters on a ship that's tilting one way and then the other.

The same thing can happen in a school. One teacher says, "These are my rules, and if you break them, you'll suffer the consequences." Another teacher is so loosey-goosey kids can feel there are no rules. Thriving in either scenario is impossible.

Kids can survive in both environments, whether at home or school. They will be more comfortable in one style or another.

**Surviving and comfort isn't what we're after.
It's thriving and growth.**

Modeling an empowerment mindset is one of the greatest gifts you can provide your kids and students. It's one thing to desire an empowerment mindset and quite another to have one. This book will help you move from desire to completion, and I applaud you for choosing to become a parent or educator of confidence, effectiveness, and empathy.

Pull on your work boots! In the next chapter, we're going to step into a demanding job site!

Key Points & Tips

◊ You're the project manager of this brain remodel, but you can't fire the contractors or the inspector. Your job is to maintain a vision for what adolescence and adulthood can look like!

◊ Communicate your vision, expectations, and desires with clarity.

◊ It's not a matter of "if" the unexpected will occur; only when. Expect the unexpected!

◊ Role-playing how you would respond if your child experiences or causes a difficult or devastating event or relationship doesn't mean you secretly think those things will happen. It can be a way of preparing yourself for life's possibilities and having courageous humility to accept there's very little in your control.

◊ Going through adolescence isn't a choice. It's a life stage, no different than infancy or old age. We only get to decide how we're going to get through those seasons, not whether we're going to.

◊ It's when adolescents act like they least need you that they most need you. Adolescents are often confusing to themselves. Pay attention to their cues for engagement while knowing they may not know what they need themselves or how to ask for it.

◊ While the physiological changes of adolescence should never excuse poor choices or behavior, it should be cause for you to maintain a heart of empathy, a mindset of confidence, and a commitment to effectiveness.

◊ Adolescence marks the stage of "no return." There's no going back to the naivety of childhood or not having to deal with one's sexuality or recognizing the world is more complex than previously thought.

◊ Grief is a part of adolescence. There aren't just gains; there are losses. Adolescents might not even be aware of this grief. Initiate conversations about the losses of childhood. Point out that longing for "simpler times" isn't just about returning to childhood; it's a spiritual hunger to return to the "Garden" when people knew nothing of sin.

◊ Adolescence isn't a disease in need of a cure.

◊ Two perspectives to reject:

1) Fear sets children up for failure by instilling a panicked mindset and focusing on all the potential problems, conflict, and dangers.

2) Helplessness sets children up for failure by fostering a powerless mindset. "I'm just at the whims of whatever happens to my body."

Worth Exploring

Dr. Kevin Leman is the author of over 45 books on parenting, marriage, and family life and hosts a podcast, "Have a New Kid by Friday."

One of his principles is: "Empathy with consequences," and I highly recommend learning more through his books and podcast about how to implement this principle in practical ways.

Learn more at https://birthorderguy.com/

Take Action

Two of the best books to help your adolescent adopt an attitude of gratitude and empowerment are below. These are true stories of adolescents who faced incredible challenges, both in the United States and internationally. Consider listening as a family on audio. As always, read first to assess the appropriateness for your child.

Warriors Don't Cry: A Searing Memoir of the Battle to Integrate Little Rock's Central High
by Melba Pattillo Beals

I Am Malala: The Girl Who Stood Up for Education and Was Shot by the Taliban
by Malala Yousafzai and Patricia McCormick

Personal Application & Reflection

Chapter 3

It's Going to Get Messy

Have you ever been through a home renovation project? It's messy. It's complicated. It's seldom on schedule or on budget. This is a perfect parallel to adolescence when the brain undergoes a massive physiological remodel. This isn't the equivalent of updating bathroom faucets or giving the kitchen a "face lift" with new paint and fixtures. This is a "tear it down to the studs, replace the wiring, and oh yeah, while you're at it, could you remove the load-bearing wall to open up the space between the kitchen and family room?

Mark Twain stated, "When I was a boy of fourteen, my father was so ignorant I could hardly stand to have the old man around. But when I got to be twenty-one, I was astonished at how much the old man had learned in seven years." Going back further, Shakespeare mused in *The Winter's Tale*, "I would there were no age between sixteen and three-and-twenty, or that youth would sleep out the rest; for there is nothing in the between but getting wenches with child, wronging the ancientry, stealing, fighting."

These observations coincide nicely with modern neuroscience.

Research shows the brain's remodel takes about ten years to complete, beginning around 12-14 and ending around 22-24.

This is why I'm not going to refer to "teens" or "teenagers." There's nothing magical about age "13" or "18," and although legal considerations change considerably at age 18, this brain remodel doesn't just conveniently align with that legally significant age.

Girls, on average, enter and exit adolescence one to two years earlier than boys, and we'll come back to the significance of that, especially in education, later on.

If you've ever been part of a remodel project, you know life cannot carry on as usual. Whether that's moving out of a house or washing dishes in the bathroom sink and eating off paper plates, flexibility is a necessity. As a parent, when you have a child enter adolescence, you will have to adapt your practices if you want to be successful. If you're an educator and you're experienced teaching younger children or adults, you can't just bring the same methodology to different content and expect good outcomes. We don't want to stand on the street and bemoan the messiness and the noise but rather step into the role as the empowered project manager as a parent and an assistant as an educator.

What makes this remodel such a momentous operation?

During infancy and childhood the brain engages in a massive neural connection process. Estimates range from

30,000 to 1,000,000 neural connections per second form in the first three years of life!

Imagine a machine connecting 30,000 Legos per second for three years!

These connections continue to be formed throughout childhood, leaving a person with trillions of connections by the beginning of adolescence -- more than the number of stars in the Milky Way galaxy! At one point the brain says, "Hmmm, I need to remove some of these connections and make the ones I keep more efficient." It does this through a process called myelination. Myelin is a fatty and protein substance that sheaths around nerves, similar to how electrical wires are encased in a protective skin. Some connections are removed and others reinforced.

The myelin that coats these connections not only preserves them but speeds them up. It's like a highway department saying, "We're going to shut down these side streets which get little, if any, use, and we're going to concentrate on making our main roads more efficient." The cost of this remodel is plasticity.

The brain remodel exchanges adaptability for efficiency.

In the limbic system of our brain we have the controls for memory and emotion, and it is highly integrated with the endocrine system which controls hormones. In the front part of our brain is the prefrontal cortex which houses complex cognitive thinking, personality, social behavior, and decision-making abilities. The general contractor in charge of this brain remodel project places myelinating the connections between these two parts of the brain towards the end of the job.

Really let that sink in.

The myelination between these two rooms is what takes place at the end of the remodel. In one room we have memory, emotion, and hormone controls, and in the other we have complex thinking, decision making, social behavior, and personality, and the general contractor says, "We're going to open up that wall and connect those two rooms last."

That doesn't mean nothing is happening in these rooms until then. These rooms are undergoing their own renovations. Part of this process is deciding what's going to stay and what's going to go. Just as house designers and contractors walk through a house and say, "Those fixtures have got to go. Tear them out and toss them in the dumpster. We'll keep the cabinets, but we'll give them a total face lift with new paint and hardware." In the same way, the brain is looking at its trillions of connections and saying, "Don't need those. Don't need those. That one we want to keep, so let's get some myelin over here."

These rooms aren't just lying dormant; they're undergoing transformation, but they don't get connected until the later part of adolescence. This is why you end up with a kid swinging from one hand at the top of a water tower!

The adrenaline hormones in one part of the brain aren't connected to cognitive, long-term thinking in the next room until the last phase of the remodel.

So much of the frustration of parents and educators with adolescents is this disconnect between the decisions being made today and the outcomes of those choices in the future. There is a brain-based disparity between what an adolescent has the capacity to do physically and cognitively.

That doesn't mean they have no decision-making abilities.

It does mean we cannot, as individuals or a society, abdicate the role of adult leadership.

In our society that glorifies youth, not only in the world but often in the church – that can be a hard thing to do. But hard is not impossible.

In house remodels, the general contractor hires out sub-contractors and they have specific job assignments. That's what happens in the adolescent brain remodel job. Get ready to meet the first of three primary subcontractors in Chapter 4.

Key Points & Tips

◊ This is a major physiological remodel, not a weekend update. It takes about ten years, beginning around age 12-14 and ending around ages 22-24. Girls enter and exit, on average, adolescence about two years prior to boys.

◊ Melatonin (the sleep hormone) kicks in about 60-90 minutes later in an adolescent than a child or adult. Welcome to late night conversations, not only during high school but college. They'll be alert and awake later than you at night and want to sleep in later in the morning. If you're not available late at night for conversations, you will miss golden opportunities. This doesn't mean every night, but it means some every week. Mornings are not, on average, prime time for conversations, but each child's energy wiring is different.

◊ The brain will decide what neural connections to keep and what to cut based on what's being used now, not based on past likes or future needs. If your child always showed a great love for exploring outside and now decides to spend all their time indoors playing video games or being on-line, the brain won't say, "Hey, those outside experiences were great!" Instead, it will conclude those activities no longer serve much of a purpose.

◊ Memory and emotion are highly integrated with the endocrine (or hormone control) system. Adolescents will become both better forgetters and rememberers. Their memory and emotions aren't entirely hormonally related, but are to a large degree.

◊ Hormones and emotions will go from 0-60 faster than complex cognitive thinking.

◊ Not reacting to the initial words or behaviors will help you assess what your adolescent truly thinks and feels. If you react too intensely too quickly, they may stay embedded in their initial stance out of defensiveness. A little distance can leave room for a lot of adjustments.

◊ Adolescents need help knowing how to verbally express emotions. Expand your emotional language vocabulary beyond "happy" and "sad" and "angry" and "calm" and use these words to express yourself.

◊ Adolescents need help knowing how to physically express emotions. Physical activity can help regulate emotions before and after they're experienced. How? Physically active bodies release "feel good" chemicals which empower a person to have better reactions to difficult or disappointing events.

◊ Model and instruct how to appropriately release "feel bad" chemicals. Think of practices which will work throughout life. Going into the back yard and screaming might work if you live in an isolated area. Not going to go over too well in a suburb or city.

◊ Be intentional about discovering their personality, abilities, vulnerabilities, and struggles. Be your child's best student!

Worth Exploring

The body expends tremendous energy on the adolescent brain remodel process. Energy is work, and work requires fuel. Adolescents require increased sleep and excellent nutrition.

Culture isn't your friend when it comes to food.

Adolescents won't thrive on pizza and soda alone. Good intentions don't make up for bad diets. Invest some time in creating food plans filled with so much excellence it will help offset the lousy. Small replacements of junk with a better alternative are wins. In adolescence, every win counts!

To understand the different innate rhythms of high-mid-low energy, consider one or both of the following books. Although not geared towards adolescence, you'll benefit both as a parent of an adolescent and an individual!

At Your Best:
How to Get Time, Energy, and Priorities Working in Your Favor
by Carey Nieuwhof

When: The Scientific Secrets of Perfect Timing
by Daniel H. Pink

Take Action

It can be difficult and frustrating to know when an adolescent has forgotten something because of this physiological brain remodel or is using that as an excuse. Help them and spare yourself needless struggles!

The brain is essentially lazy and doesn't want to be bothered storing any more information than it has to. It would rather be looking for something new and exciting!

Help adolescents find and experiment with organization systems until they discover one that suits their style and needs. It might be as simple as a large dry-erase calendar or a sophisticated app. (Consider the ramifications of tying their organization system to a smart phone.)

If they balk, try the "Baseball" tactic. Tell them, "Three

strikes and you're out of excuses or reasons not to bring some order into your life. Your forgetfulness or disorganization creates problems for others, and maturity owns our impact on others." Train adolescents to see the height of maturity is not independence but owning our interdependence!

Personal Application & Reflection

Chapter 4

That's Just Dope

Three main subcontractors are at work in the adolescent brain renovation. Two tend to be buddies, while the third fluctuates between friend and adversary. Let's meet the first contractor, Mr. Reward.

Your initial impression may not be favorable. Mr. Reward appears superficial and selfish. But the brain needs a blueprint, and a major factor in deciding what to demolish and what to build is "What's in my best interest?" Since long-term analytical thinking is still developing, Mr. Reward wants a quick and easy-to-use measuring tool, and this turns out to be dopamine.

Sometimes referred to as the "Feel Good" transmitter, dopamine is a neurochemical involved in memory and motivation. During adolescence the quantity of dopamine sensors increase and become more sensitive than they ever will be again in life.

This is one dominant reason people can often recall with

such imagery, precision, and emotions the music, food, friendships, books, clothes, movies, or experiences from their adolescent years.

Life is experienced difficulty during adolescence. It's not just about perception. The body experiences taste, touch, smell, sight, and sound differently than childhood or adulthood. People like to think they remember the music of their adolescence because "it was so much better back then." But that's not the reason they can recall the lyrics 30 years later. It's because the music imprinted in their brain's "wet cement" phase.

Have you seen the Wendy's commercial from the 1980's with the infamous line, "Where's the beef?" If not, you can find it on-line. Adolescent brains are begging, "Where's the dopamine?" The desire for dopamine doesn't end with adolescence. It remains important throughout life. But during adolescence, the appetite explodes. This physiological craving, not just character, prompts many destructive behaviors.

Dopamine receptors are almost a perfect molecular match for alcohol and tobacco. A mouse click can begin a sexual enslavement. The adolescent brain is incredibly vulnerable to drug addiction.

There's a physiological factor in why almost no one engages in criminal activity for the first time past the age of 25. Very few addictions begin past the age of 25 when a person had no prior exposure or experience, whether it's chemical, sexual, or behavioral. Sadly, so much of what is bad for us also feeds the appetite for dopamine.

It can be tempting to see dopamine as the enemy of adolescence, but the potential dangers don't invalidate the need for rewarding experiences, because these are critical to move into a whole adult life.

What would the world be if no one had an intense drive to discover or create new things? How small our lives would be if we didn't desire new experiences or relationships. Just like a hammer can be used for demolition and construction, Mr. Reward can tear down or build up.

What triggers dopamine? Anything that produces a feeling of reward and that means seeking what's new.

The adolescent brain asks, "How do I know if something will be rewarding unless I try it?" A fifteen year old isn't going to get a dopamine drip from riding their bike up and down the same street as they did when they were five. But bungee jump on their bike off a cliff? That's new. Let's try it!

It's important to remember that "new" is what the adolescent defines it to be, not adults.

For example, a junior starting Algebra II is, technically, beginning a new class. But depending on her interests, not her character, her brain may not register the class as "new." It's just more math. Having a new teacher may signal her brain to consider this class as "new," but if the instructor's style and curriculum is similar to what's been previously experienced, Mr. Reward says, "Oh, same ol, same ol' here" and looks elsewhere to fill his order of "new."

Both parents and educators can wonder, "Why don't these kids care about their grades?" But from the adolescent brain's perspective, there's nothing new about grades. These are old news. They've been getting grades for years. It's a good reason for schools to consider adopting different assessment methodology during high school. Tossing out grades entirely may not be a practical option, but you can consider adding supplemental assessment protocols.

The time between action and reward has a direct relationship with motivation. A student may experience a dopamine drip when they study on Tuesday, take an exam on Wednesday, and see an "A" on Friday. But dopamine will snore all through, "You need to get good grades so you can go to a good college and have a good life." The time between action and reward is just too great.

We want people to learn delayed gratification. But we can also harness this brain craving for short-term rewards during adolescence. Mr. Reward gets his work orders filled through other dopamine triggers such as Likes on Instagram; text message pings; and social media interactions. Every time a child's phone dings or lights up with a notification, it's telling them, "Someone wants to connect with you. Someone liked your story. Someone messaged you. Here's someone you should follow." Dopamine is triggered.

When we consider the increase in numbers of receptors and sensitivity to dopamine, watching kids walk around with their cell phones is analogous to adults walking around with an IV drip or oxygen tube.

And that's on the mild end. Consider this. Cocaine triggers the same neural pathways releasing dopamine as seeing someone "liked" your social media reel. It may not be to the same degree, but it's the same pathway. Certainly it would be unethical and immoral for scientists to conduct research to quantify "How many TikTok 'likes' equals one gram of cocaine?" But smart phone addiction is real. And like most addictions, a person doesn't become an addict overnight. And like most addictions, the person who insists the loudest "I don't have a problem" is usually the one with a problem! It's often the people closest to the addict who are in denial or are, even with good intentions, enabling them.

But health is not the absence of addiction. There are plenty of people who are not alcoholics or drug addicts who are not healthy. Just like we wouldn't declare a home remodeling project a great success because the contractors didn't destroy the entire kitchen, we don't want to measure success for our adolescents by whether they reach "addict" status in any area of life, including technology.

This brings us to the issue of video games, especially for young men. There is so much wrapped up in this issue that I can't deal with all of it in this book. But I would be remiss to not address this at all.

Video gaming floods the body with dopamine – some studies suggest as much as sex or amphetamines.

It's not like turning on the water faucet, filling a cup, and turning off the faucet. It's like turning on the dopamine tap and just letting it run. But the body and brain have limits about what it can absorb or produce, and eventually something crashes or loses its sensitivity and requires more and more before it says, "Okay, job's done for the day. We can all go home now."

Video gaming also meets the brain's craving for unpredictability and a fast pace. The reward system of video gaming operates the very same way as slot machines. "This time I'll reach that level. I'll beat that other player." When an adolescent sits down to play most video games -- and this has nothing to do with its rating, content, or violence level -- they are, in effect, sitting at a slot machine. It's not the promise of money that draws people to gambling; it's the hope of a reward. The less time between the action and the reward the better; the more fast-paced the better; and the more visually engaging -- especially for males who are more wired for visual stimulation -- the better. During adolescence, Mr. Reward never wears out his welcome, although he can wear down the brain.

Technology usage can quickly put Mr. Reward in charge of the brain's remodel. Mr. Reward is the contractor you want on your side. You can't fire him. If you try to do that, he'll just go sulk in the corner and wait until you're out of sight and then kick it into high gear.

Remember the overarching process that's going on. It's not just about the brain craving dopamine.

The brain is literally eliminating neural connections it has decided has no value and wrapping with myelin those connections labeled as high priority. One of the ways it decides what's going to be preserved and what's going to be

eliminated is what's now in use. Not what was important at age five or ten but now.

Maybe you're feeling a bit overwhelmed at this point. Don't despair. Take a deep breath. Remember what I talked about earlier. Your goal is to build your confidence, effectiveness, and understanding. You are making progress by just educating yourself about this astounding process. So hang in there. Get ready to meet Mr. Reward's good buddy, Risk, and sometimes pal, sometimes adversary, Miss Relationship, in the next chapter.

Key Points & Tips

◊ One of the primary contractors is Mr. Reward. He appears superficial but is actually necessary for a meaningful life. Remember what God promises us when we get to heaven – "Well done, good and faithful servant." That's a reward!

◊ Mr. Reward feeds primarily on dopamine which is both a hormone and powerful neural transmitter.

◊ The music, food, literature, and relational experiences leave a profound imprint on the mind because dopamine receptors multiply in number and intensity during adolescence.

◊ Adolescents are incredibly vulnerable to drug, alcohol, sexual, and tobacco addictions, not only because of peer pressure but physical cravings.

◊ Adolescents crave "new," but "new" as defined by them, not others.

◊ Time between action and reward has a direct relationship with motivation. Study hard today to get into a good college or job years from now is just too big of a jump. Even students highly motivated to be accepted into a specific college or program have short-term reward goals: earning 100% on a test; achieving a 4.0 GPA for the semester, etc.

◊ The less time between action and reward the better.

◊ It's impossible for social media and dopamine to break up.

◊ Expecting the adolescent to be able to assess how well they can or are handling technology is like asking the fox to guard the hen house and then leaving the coop door wide open. Their brain has a gravity-like pull for "reward, reward, reward!"

◊ Very little in life can offer the same visual stimulation, short time between risk and reward, and fast pace of video games. The brain will create expectations about investment of time and return on reward and transfer these expectations into other situations.

Health is not the absence of addictions.

Worth Exploring

Although not specifically about video gaming, one resource to begin examining the effects of screen-based technology is:

Irresistible: The Rise of Addictive Technology and the Business of Keeping Us Hooked
by Adam Alter

I feel your pain!

As mom to five competitive sons, I understand the challenges of video games! When a friend gifted us with a Nintendo 64 system (hey, that was something back in the day), my sons were ecstatic -- and eventually obsessed. Seriously. I tried every imaginable schedule, plan, and system to let them enjoy this gift without it turning them into automatons. Nothing worked. It was like a children's version of *The Stepford Wives.* Eventually, the book, **Failure to Connect** by Jane Healy cinched my decision to keep video gaming only for special occasions.

Having one kid upset with you is unpleasant. Having all five mad at you is a nightmare. (Spoiler alert: Everyone survived, and we're still talking.) I invited my older kids to read the book for themselves. (Arguing with research isn't nearly as appealing to adolescents as facing off with a parent.)

I don't advocate a one-size-fits-all-solution. I do believe there's an obligation every parent has: making a thoroughly informed decision. Loads more research has been conducted since Jane Healy's book, and besides, there's still this thing called common sense.

Does it feel right to watch boys (and girls) sit for extended periods, rotating joysticks or clicking on keyboards? Adolescents who, a few generations past, would be herding cows, felling trees, bucking #100 hay bales, and helping construct a barn.

Count the opportunity cost. Every "yes" is a "no" to something else. What are all the "no" activities that an adolescent could be doing instead? Stewarding our lives isn't only about avoiding "bad" or "wrong" actions. It's about filling them with what is best.

There's too much at stake to naively think, "It's just a phase" when it comes to gaming. You wouldn't say this if they were sitting on the sofa snorting cocaine. Be informed. Be courageous. Be a good role model. Their brain will thank you ... eventually.

Take Action

When my two nephews wanted a gaming system, their dad required them to write two papers: one detailing why this was a good idea; the other explaining why it wasn't. In addition, they were required to outline the conditions for use if they got one. Their guidelines were tougher than those their father would have implemented. They got the system.

Make video gaming and screen time a privilege earned, not a right claimed. For example:

Two hours of reading = 1 hour of game/screen time.

Three hours of extra chores = 1 hour of game/screen time.

If they complain, remind them of the work-to-rest ratio God established for people: Six days of work to one day of rest.

Anything under a 6/1 ratio is generous!

Require reading one book about the impact of gaming and screen-based technology. This isn't punishment; it's teaching them to take ownership of their choices and make informed decisions.

Rewards: Yes? No? Maybe?

It's impossible to override the brain's craving for dopamine during adolescence and preference for satisfying that appetite with short-term rewards. Yet, maturity requires delayed gratification. What to do?

Remember, this is like a home remodel: You move from idea to plan to implementation, with several mini accomplishments leading to the finished project.

Demolition completed? Check! (Literally and figuratively.) Cabinets and appliances ordered and installed? Check. Enough funds will be withheld until the entire undertaking is completed to insure the contractor doesn't decide to skip town and leave you with no flooring and live wires hanging out of outlet boxes. You pay for work completed, not promised, and definitely not just for showing up on the job site.

Take this approach with your adolescent. Getting out of bed is like showing up for work. Completing chores and homework on time with enough quality to pass inspection might be reward-worthy. "Might" is a key word, because the goal isn't to reward *every* behavior; it's to choose some as leverage to help build personal responsibility.

If everything gets rewarded, you risk raising an adult with

an entitlement mentality which is like having a toddler in a big body wielding a jack hammer. If you're not involved in creating opportunities for rewards, your child will seek these apart from you.

This doesn't mean rewarding only activities which happen at home; this includes interests supported by you. Athletics; fine arts; paid employment; entrepreneurial enterprises.

Here are three ways to approach rewards:

1. Keep rewards from becoming expectations by putting them on a time limit. "I know you're working hard to save enough money to purchase a new saddle for your horse. I'd like to help you accomplish this goal. This month, instead of you paying 100% of the cost of gas to go back and forth to work, I'm going to split the cost 50/50 and help you reach your goal even faster. This is a limited time offer and is dependent on you continuing to be responsible in other areas. I know you will be, and I'm excited to see what saddle you're going to purchase." This way cost-sharing of gas is tied to a measurable goal which your child has an internal motivation to achieve and is time limited.

2. Solicit ideas from your adolescent on how rewards might help motivate them in an area where they're struggling. Do we ever outgrow the desire to have outside incentives to accomplish a tough goal? Building willpower and discipline is a process, not an event. Demanding an adolescent (or adult) do the right thing because it's the right thing is an ideal worth working towards, but it's a process. As humans, we are simultaneously incredibly capable and astoundingly vulnerable. Embracing this tension is one of the best ways you can equip young people for adulthood.

3. Think beyond cash. Time with friends; time off from chores; a special outing with one or all family members; getting to decide the dinner menus for a week; making their favorite meal; tickets to a concert, show, or event; guitar lessons; skydiving coupon; permission for a multi-day bike trip with a friend; trail ride for a horse lover; curfew extension; use of a vehicle; whatever works for you and is meaningful for them!

Remember rewards aren't implicitly selfish. In the Bible, Hebrews chapter 11, verse 6 states it's impossible to please God if you don't believe he rewards people who diligently seek him. Whoa! Here and in other parts of Scripture God models the relationship between action and reward is a good one!

Personal Application & Reflection

Chapter 5

It's Risky & Complicated

If you've been wondering why "alligators" is part of this book's subtitle, you're about to find out!

Mr. Reward has a pal. His name is Risk. He's the contractor who shows up and speculates, "If we moved this here ..." and Mr. Reward says, "Couldn't hurt to try!" One author compared the adolescent brain to a car with a gas pedal and no brake. Tragically, it is often major collisions which end risk-taking behavior. But it is also Risk who can motivate students to audition for a new role; try out for the team; ask out the girl; reveal themselves in a writing assignment; join the mission trip; run for student council.

As a rule, adolescents are more reward motivated than risk averse.

In other words, their brains do a calculation – often without consulting the prefrontal cortex with its cognitive thinking skills which assess long term consequence. The result? A small possibility of reward is greater than a large guaranteed quantity of risk. Hence, let's swing from one hand at the top of a water tower. Sure, the risk of falling is death or life-long paralysis. But adolescent math calculates the reward of accomplishing something so dangerous is greater than the risk -- including the possibility of death.

Again, we have to see through the eyes of the adolescent. For us, we can say, "What did you gain by climbing a water tower? Admission into college? A new car? Did a job result from that escapade, and now you're going to get paid to be a water tower climber?" But that's because our prefrontal cortex is fully functioning – hopefully!

Now, some of you are probably thinking, "My son would never do that because he's too obedient and knows the consequences that kind of tomfollery would be severe." And you have a valid point. My son did have enough awareness to know he shouldn't have been climbing water towers which is why I didn't find out about it until his wedding reception. Let me reiterate a point from a previous chapter:

Understanding this brain remodel isn't the same as excusing adolescents from poor choices. They're not to be treated as a victim of this process but as an owner of this process.

Now Risk and Mr. Reward have an understanding. Risk must stay in the sweet spot. If Mr. Reward feels his expectations can't be met, he'll bail. If it's not risky enough, he'll decline out of boredom. Adolescents need enough of a challenge to engage, but if they don't see any way to reach the finish line, the brain advises, "Don't waste your energy; a reward is impossible." And if it's not challenging enough, the brain yawns, "Don't bother; the reward is insignificant. It's not worth my time. I'll go look for something else."

Just like Mr. Reward can become a tyrant on this brain remodel job site, Risk can, too. But you can't fire either one of them. And placating them is just a softer way to turn them into tyrants. But engaging and winning them over to be used for good is what you're after. Now sometimes that will include confronting and correcting them. It also means being willing to let them fail, because often failure is our best teacher.

For educators, a legitimate thought at this point may be, "I'm not sure about the Risk and Reward relationship. I could promise pizza for life and still have students unwilling to raise their hand and answer one True/False question in class, much less pole-vault out of their comfort zone."

This is where a third contractor gets involved. Miss Relationship. She complicates everything. Adults process people interactions primarily with the prefrontal cortex while adolescents engagements default to the limbic system. Remember, the prefrontal cortex houses complex cognitive thinking, social interactions, personality, decision-making skills, while the limbic system is concerned with emotions and memory and closely integrated with the endocrine system which regulates hormones.

The complications of relationships multiply where romance is concerned. Guess what studies show about this situation?

It takes about 18 months for the brain to settle down enough that it begins to examine the relationship more from the prefrontal cortex and less from the limbic system.

The goal isn't to exclude the limbic system's influence but to balance it with the prefrontal cortex's input.

Adolescents are notoriously inept at correctly identifying other people's emotions. Young children can be better at accurately identifying other people's emotions. So even if a child was adept at this task, that ability is going to get muddled during adolescence. That doesn't mean the ability drops to zero. It does mean the margin for error increases, and while we don't want to write off any adolescent's observations about others and their intentions towards them, neither do we want to just accept everything at face value.

"Maybe, honey, when your friend said that, she wasn't as upset as you felt. Let's investigate a little further." The opposite can also happen. "Hey, kiddo, I'm not sure she's as crazy about you as you are about her. Of course she should be! Maybe give it a little bit more time before asking her out?"

Now, because we must live in the world we're dealt, not the one we want, we can't avoid the reality of sexual predators and abusers, whether on-line or in person and whether in a family, church, school, neighborhood, or peer group.

Never diminish an adolescent's concern (or yours) about someone's conduct or intentions towards them when there is anything that suggests a "secretive and special" or a "secretive and threatening" vibe.

This is true regardless of the genders involved.

Not only do adolescents misread a lot of other people's emotions, they're not exceptionally skilled at knowing how to handle other people's emotions. This isn't just true for the stereotypical socially awkward kid with the uncanny ability to always say the wrong thing. It's also true for the adolescent who is empathetic and popular. They may be learning to please and placate at the expense of not knowing when and how to challenge and confront.

Again, this doesn't mean adolescents have zero emotional intelligence. It does mean we don't assume the socially awkward kid will just outgrow it or the has-it-all-together-kid really does. We remain intentional about modeling and teaching emotional intelligence skills.

When Miss Relationship is on site for the remodel, Risk either slouches into the corner or leaps to the center of the room.

Statistically, the number of accidents or activities like robbing convenience stores, racing 100 mph down the highway, drinking, taking drugs, or swinging from one arm at the top of a water tower is not high when there's only one adolescent involved. But you put two or more together, and the dynamic changes immediately.

Now, the alligator. The picture on the book's back cover is from an incident at a site outside of Charleston, South Carolina. I was attending a photography conference, and another participant told me about a wild mama alligator and her clutch of babies at the end of a trail along a rookery. I spent some time taking photographs with a super-zoom telephoto lens, and when I finished and was walking away, I passed two young women. Probably in their early twenties, they weren't part of the photography tour, but I thought they might like to stop and observe the mama and baby alligators.

Some things, I later realized, are better left unsaid. At first, the two gals approached with great caution and quiet, remaining an appropriate distance away. And then, as the minutes ticked by and the alligator remained unmoved, they began to get a little more "adventurous." I began to get a little more scared and agitated. They weren't young kids, so I didn't feel it was appropriate to go and shoosh them down the trail. But I did occasionally look back from my new position to check on them. That's when I saw a sight that totally unnerved me.

One of the girls had laid down on her back, with her head no more than five feet away from this wild mama alligator watching over her clutch of babies. She took a selfie. Her friend looked a little nervous, but she giggled and went along with this irrationality. She wasn't pulling on Ms. Selfie-Stupid and saying, "No! You can't do this! It's not safe!"

Adolescents are far more likely to act rashly, without thought, when two or more get together.

I doubt the girl who risked decapitation by angry alligator would have been so inclined if she'd been alone.

She truly was risking her life. In one lunge and one bite, that mama gator would have clamped her powerful jaws around Ms. Selfie-Stupid's head and drug her into the water. What was her friend and I supposed to do?

Why did she do it? Relationships. Risk. Reward. She had a friend along to share the experience. (Relationship) Great risk, according to adolescent math, was worth the small reward. What was the reward? Attention and approval. No doubt she immediately or soon after posted her photo, and there was her reward: Everyone (Miss Relationship again) on social media could applaud her risky endeavor. And remember we talked about the shorter the interval of time between action and the reward, the better? Technology has shrunk that time span to seconds.

If Ms. Selfie-Stupid had been alone, without a phone or camera, and with no social media accounts to post a photo to, the idea to get so close to a protective wild animal and position herself in such an unbelievably dangerous position wouldn't have even occurred to her. Risk, relationship, and reward have a significant impact not only on *how* adolescents think -- but *what* they think!

In addition to technology shrinking the time span between risk and reward to almost zero, it has also increased the presence of "peers" to near infinity. "Friends" have been redefined to be anyone with whom there's a digital connection without any need to have even laid eyes on the person, much less spent time with them.

Once upon a time, adolescents had a built-in separation from their peers as well as adults and celebrities. When school was over, peers were gone or limited to those you desired and had opportunity to be with. The lines between adults and kids were fairly clear, and engagement with celebrities and "influencers" required a newspaper, magazine, movie ticket, entrance to a stadium, or well-connected great aunt. Today, that's gone.

Make no mistake, the virtual presence of peers can be just as influential as their physical proximity, and in certain ways, even more potent.

There is tremendous power in writing. The brain engages with written material very differently than visual or auditory information. In a culture that's fixated on content and considers the formats interchangeable, that does not serve us well. We need engagement with written material that requires time and a deep analysis to be and become our best selves.

However, when we move from verbal communication to purely written communication, we reduce our tool selection to just two: words and punctuation. That's it. And even if we expand that to include emoji's and GIF's, we've still given up the power tools of intonation, body language, facial expressions, volume, and tone of voice.

Therefore, when an adolescent has another person virtually present and is only communicating through words, abbreviations, emoji's, and gifs, the possibility for misinterpretation – either favorably or unfavorably – flies off the charts.

Miss Relationship has a lot of potential, and we cannot flourish without her. But during adolescence, her enthusiasm greatly exceeds her experience, and the result is she causes or contributes to many on-the-job injuries.

There are few days an adolescent doesn't experience an

emotional hammer on the thumb if not a sledgehammer to the heart. Even if they make it through a school day without an injury, there's likely one waiting for them on a device with a screen somewhere. There's no longer built-in recovery time between blows.

This impacts students at home, school, church, work, everywhere. Where do they go to have a "safe place" where they can recover from the inevitable blows of other adolescents, not to mention the constant battering of a dark world filled with evil? Adults must create these places for them, even if they protest and claim, "I'm fine."

Gender differences create complications in the classroom and can set up divisive family relationships between brothers and sisters. If you recall from earlier, boys enter and exit adolescence about one to two years later than girls. That's on average, and there will always be outliers.

A high school class can easily have students who vary by four years in their brain maturation process, and typically it's the boys who are "behind."

Let's consider this for a moment. By 11th grade, an average boy has spent four or more years trailing the average girl in his class. And he knows it. If we remember the understanding Mr. Reward and Risk have – to not try when there's not a likelihood of success – and we add in the new sensitivity to girls, it's understandable why some boys resort to doing enough to get by.

I'm not saying it's acceptable; I am saying it's understandable.

And at home, parents can exacerbate this by commenting, "Your sister didn't have a problem with that. Your sister didn't struggle like you. Your sister didn't act that way when she was your age. Your sister..." Blah, blah, blah.

Much research shows kids in the early ages of adolescence fare much better when they are in the same-gender schools. Now I'm not advocating for a return to that, although I'm not opposed to it on a matter of principle. It is critical, as both parents and educators, we deal with adolescents as individuals, not by comparing them, especially one gender to the other.

Girls have their own set of vulnerabilities. Boys tend to act out; girls tend to turn inward. Boys tend to ask, "What's wrong with you?" Girls favor asking, "What's wrong with me?"

Boys lean toward valuing appearing successful, and if they don't see being a great student as possible, they'll be successful as a "poor" student which school and perhaps parents punish. Girls tend to value acceptance, and they can pursue perfectionism as a means of gaining approval which school and home rewards.

Girls can also feel they have to choose between academic excellence and adult approval or academic mediocrity and peer acceptance, especially from boys. And both genders struggle mightily, even if silently, with how to navigate the complexities sexual maturation brings.

Whew. Take time to digest this. Let it soak in. Don't be

discouraged or fearful. You're in a process of building your confidence, effectiveness, and empathy. That takes time and sometimes means, "I need to step back and let the dust settle." When you're ready for the next chapter, there's one more team member on this amazing brain remodel project you need to meet.

Key Points & Tips

◊ Adolescents are more reward motivated than risk adverse. A small possibility of reward is greater than a large quantity of risk. Reward has to be seen through the adolescent's eyes, not adults.

◊ Reward needs enough risk to be motivated to engage, but if expectations can't be met (through the adolescent's eyes), he'll bail. Too little, and he'll decline out of boredom.

◊ Placating adolescents is just a softer way to turn them into tyrants. Engage, don't placate.

◊ Adolescents must be allowed to fail.

◊ Young children can be better at identifying other people's emotions than adolescents. Adolescents need help correctly interpreting other people's emotions and behaviors. They tend to overreact or under-react.

◊ Adolescents are incredibly vulnerable to manipulation and abuse, especially because they often feel so powerful. **Pay attention to anyone in their circle who seems "secretive and special" or "secretive and threatening."**

◊ Adolescents struggle with being able to handle other people's emotions. This isn't just true for the socially awkward kid but for those who are empathetic and popular. Adolescents who learn to please and placate others can develop relational patterns just as damaging in the long run as being withdrawn and combative or alone and awkward.

◊ Adolescents need adults to give them language for their and others' emotions and teach and model emotional intelligence skills.

◊ Social media can be one-way, consumer vs. provider, and still feel like a "connection" has happened. Even when it's two-way, it's still limited and both people control when, how, and if they'll respond. To prepare for mature relationships, it's critical adolescents experience many face to face conversations that are two-way and where they don't control the subject, length, or purpose.

◊ With the constant engagement technology allows, adults must create emotional "safe" places, not only in response to hurtful encounters but to proactively limit them.

◊ In the classroom, a brain maturation process can easily vary by four years, and it's usually the boys who are "behind." This can account for why so many boys give up on academics in high school. It's not that their egos can't handle girls outperforming them; it's that their hearts can't. Watch the comparisons – at home and in the classroom between males and females.

Worth Exploring

We tend to have far more negative labels for emotions than positive. **Angry, sad, afraid, alone, anxious, and ashamed** versus **happy, glad, upbeat, and excited.**

Give adolescents a rich emotional vocabulary. Search online for "emotional language" or "emotional vocabulary" and you'll find everything from articles to games to wall charts.

Take Action

Teach and model one or both of these frameworks to process emotions in a healthy way.

Let it RAIN:
Recognize, Allow, Inquire, Nurture

R -- Recognize. Pay attention to what your body and mindset is telling you.

A -- Allow. Trying to shut off an emotion is like trying to dam the Mississippi River. Give yourself permission to feel the emotion.

I -- Inquire. Get curious. What's caused this emotion? Is it something I often, regularly, or rarely feel? What types of situations cause this response?

N -- Nurture. How can I handle this emotion in a way that's not judgmental towards myself or hurtful to someone else?

LUV

L -- Listen. This is not just hearing, but actively listening with the intent to learn and understand, not respond.

U -- Understand by asking clarifying questions instead of making assumptions.

V -- Validate the emotions another is feeling. This doesn't require agreement or apologies; it is affirming another person's experience rather than dismissing it.

(Credit to Donna Scott of https://www.donnascotttherapy.com for the LUV framework.)

Personal Application & Reflection

Chapter 6

Inspector Clouseau and You

In 1963 Metro-Goldwyn-Mayer released the film, "The Pink Panther." This movie went on to become a franchise including video games, television specials, and cartoon shows. Peter Sellers first played the role of the inept French police detective, Inspector Jacques Clouseau. He remained convinced of his abilities no matter how many times he failed, even at the most basic tasks.

The adolescent brain remodel team includes a building inspector who, in many ways, mirrors Jacques Clouseau. He has a job he's focused on doing. He wants everyone around him to trust he can get the job done all by himself. But he's constantly imperiling himself because of his refusal to listen to others.

The brain remodel inspector's job is regulation. Just like in a house remodel, the inspector sees to it that contractors are completing work according to the plans and building codes. The brain remodel inspector's job is to regulate what Mr. Reward, Risk, and Miss Relationship are doing. "Is Mr. Reward going off schedule? Is Risk way over budget? Is Miss Relationship staying in her lane?"

The problem is he's brand new for a project of this size. Like many people at their first-time job, he tends to be a bit of a know-it-all. He has, shall we say, attitude? He's heard to say things like, "I've got this." "I know what I'm doing." "Don't you trust me?"

Just like Mr. Reward, Risk, and Miss Relationship, you can't fire Inspector Clouseau. You want him on your side because at some point these four can get together and fire you. You want them as your allies. Someday this remodel will end, and you'll want to be welcomed into your child's adult life.

Adolescents like to think they are good at self-analysis. But they often confuse a growing sense of power with insight.

They are not the same thing. But if you take the approach with the Inspector that "You're a bumbling idiot, and I'm here to do your job for you," you'll ultimately fail. You must come alongside to teach self-regulation rather than trying to enforce it. Of course if the Inspector's failures are creating destructive habits and situations, you step in.

So how do you succeed as a Project Manager for this remodel? A remodel you didn't schedule, you're footing a lot of the bill for, and where your responsibility exceeds your control.

Obviously, your responsibilities vary whether you're a parent or an educator. But there are tools available to both groups.

1. **Choose a mindset of confidence.** If your home was undergoing a massive renovation and you walked in to find the general contractor wringing his hands and muttering, "I don't know what to do with this place," you would not be okay. Now you don't want a general contractor to pretend like he's not concerned the roof trusses were installed upside down. But you would want him to say, "That's not going to work. I'm going to find a way to get that fixed for you."

You would also hope that he'd be frustrated with the framing crew and would hold them accountable. In the same way, having confidence doesn't mean you're happy and carefree about everything that happens during this brain remodel. Having confidence isn't about faking it; it's all about exercising our faith. As therapist Jim Cress says, "Maturity is the willingness to embrace reality -- at all costs."

True confidence includes humility. We cannot control anyone else, and there is no formula when it comes to any human relationship that guarantees a successful outcome. Our source of confidence cannot be ourselves, nor is this confidence in outcomes. It must be in Christ and his power to preserve, redeem, and even resurrect.

We don't have confidence because we have guaranteed results as a Christian. We have confidence because we have a guaranteed Presence – the Holy Spirit.

2. **Choose effective methods.** You would not be okay with a plumber who said, "I don't know if this drain line will work or not, but I've put so much time and thought into this, I'm sure that will be sufficient." You would respond with something like, "Uh, think again, Bud. I want a toilet that flushes down the drain, not all over the floor."

Continue to pursue educating yourself about effective communication techniques, about the adolescent brain, about cultural forces affecting adolescents today. It requires work to be effective, not just good intentions. Be an educator or parent more committed to effectiveness than fitting in with your peers.

3. **Choose a mindset of understanding**. It's not like adolescents opt for a massive brain redo and schedule its start and end dates. I can feel irritated with students who seem arrogant and/or apathetic. I didn't parent through five seasons of adolescence without experiencing anger, frustration, pain, and discouragement. But think how you'd feel if a group of contractors showed up and announced they were going to begin a major remodel without your permission, and it could be a decade before they were done.

Understanding does not replace, but comes alongside of, accountability. Dr. Kevin Leman expresses this so well in his parenting approach as "Consequences with empathy." This combination is a compelling catalyst for heart change.

**Anger, irritation, and shame may modify behavior;
they do not transform hearts.**

Understanding discards labels and sees complexity. It asks, doesn't assume. It calls to; doesn't yell at. Understanding is not synonymous with caring. I can care about where a student is headed but not have empathy. Nor is understanding expressed in low expectations. It is not indulgence. Understanding with accountability is perfectly modeled in the coming of Christ to earth, the greatest expression of empathy for all time.

We are all works in progress. Let's remember adolescence isn't a culturally manufactured scheme to make our roles as parents or educators difficult, but rather is part of God's design for human development. It may be intended to refine us adults, as much as to redefine adolescents.

Key Points & Tips

◊ In the *Pink Panther* movies, Inspector Clouseau remained convinced of his abilities no matter how many times he failed. That's what the adolescent brain inspector is like. He wants everyone around him to "trust" he can do the job by himself. But he constantly imperils himself when he refuses to listen to others.

◊ Adolescents must become self-regulating to function as a mature adult. You develop this by loosening their guide ropes, a bit at a time, observing and adjusting according to how they handle the opportunities they're given.

◊ Take a cue from a former president when you hear the "Don't you trust me?" line. As Ronald Reagan put it, "Trust but verify." Trust is earned, not dispensed.

◊ When trust is broken, require the adolescent to act their way back into it. Mature people act (not promise, plead, or petition) their way back into trust.

◊ Adolescents like to think they're good at self-analysis. But self-focus isn't self-awareness. The more self-absorbed someone is, the less self-aware they are. You can't take the approach, "You're a bumbling idiot. I'll handle things for you." Rather, come alongside as a mentor, stepping in as a protector only when it's critically necessary.

Worth Exploring

Mindset matters! Romans 12:2 tells us we are transformed by the renewing of our mind. Give your adolescent a power tool for life to craft a healthy mindset.

Your New Playlist: The Student's Guide to Tapping into the Superpower of Mindset
by Jon Acuff with his daughters, L.E. Acuff and McRae Acuff
The adult version,
Soundtracks: The Surprising Solution to Overthinking
by Jon Acuff

Trust can become a thorny issue in adolescence. A fantastic resource about trust in general is:

Trust: Knowing When to Give It, When to Withhold It, How to Earn It, and How to Fix It When It Gets Broken
by Dr. Henry Cloud

Take Action

Employ adolescent self-interest for their benefit. Invite them out for dinner, shopping, a hike, concert, game -- something they enjoy. On the way there or during the activity, tell them what you are learning about the brain remodel of adolescence. Invite them to read this book. Doing so will cultivate self-awareness and give you an outside source to support your unpopular decisions. It's not that you need to justify your authority. But hey, why not take advantage of every aid available to you?!

1. Choose an attitude of humility paired with confidence.

Confidence isn't having all the answers; it's the assurance you are capable of finding them, even if it means making mistakes along the way.

2. Choose methods that work.

Be more committed to effectiveness than fitting in with your peers or maintaining the status quo or staying in your comfort zone.

3. Choose a mindset of empathy.

Understanding does not replace, but comes alongside of, accountability.

4. Choose to ask, not assume.

No one can really know the heart of another. Inquiring demonstrates humility and care.

5. Choose to cultivate integrity, not indulgence.

Empathy is not low expectations. Christ is the greatest expression of empathy of all time, and he does not have low expectations of us. Integrity balances transparency with privacy. Transparency is what leads to intimacy and accountability, two key ingredients for later relational success.

Youth's need for transparency is greater than their "right to privacy."

6. Choose to include others in your journey.

Being the parent, caregiver, or mentor of an adolescent is hard! Don't walk this journey alone. Give yourself as much support as you can -- for you and your adolescent.

Personal Application & Reflection

Chapter 7

Framing the Big Picture

In his book, *Sacred Fire*, author Ronald Rolheiser beautifully expresses the poignancy and purpose of adolescence.

"Simply put, puberty is designed by God and nature to drive us out of our homes. And puberty generally does its job, sometimes too well! It hits us with a tumult and violence that overthrows our childhood and sends us out, restless, sexually driven, full of grandiose dreams, but confused and insecure, in search of a new home, one that we build for ourselves."

Rolheiser lists the objectives of this searching: identity, acceptance, a circle of friends, intimacy, someone to marry, a vocation, a career, the right place to live, financial security, and continues

"[...] something to give us substance and meaning--in a word, searching for a home. [...] Countless expressions of longing, of heartache, of searching; but, in the end, one focus: a burning desire for a home we once had, somehow lost, and are looking for again."

"Our relationship to our home and our family takes on a different modality when we reach adolescence. Home no longer contains us as it did before, as the lure of friends, a bigger world, and bigger life begins to trump the security of our parents, family, and home. [...] A new life with seemingly unlimited opportunities now beckons us, and it is there where we want to be, impatiently so.

Puberty is a time of major disorientation, but it is also a crucial spiritual time in our lives since it is the real beginning of our personal journey toward maturity and discipleship. And given all the tumult and disorientation that puberty brings, it is a time that begs for initiation. **This time in our lives parallels the time of our infancy in terms of the need for others outside of us, elders, to help direct our energies and help protect us from ourselves."**

No matter how skilled, smart, or savvy your adolescent is, they are also desperately in need of your presence and protection. Sometimes their enemies are obvious -- addictions, criminal entanglements, sexual misconduct, self-harm, and gender chaos. Sometimes the enemies are covert -- perfectionism, people-pleasing, pride, laziness. All are destructive, just on different timelines.

However, even with all the challenges, this life season doesn't have to be driven by fear. I pray this book will help you be confident in this: the Creator in whose image we are all made is able and eager to empower you to guide your adolescent towards adulthood. His grace is greater than all your mistakes. He is an ever-present help in time of distress, and living this truth with, for, and in front of your child is the greatest gift you can ever give them.

Remember, my friend, you have an impact that is immeasurable, eternal, and irreplaceable! May you and your adolescent engage fully in God's grand story!

Bonus Insights

Ennoble, don't enable.

Ennobling empowers a person. Enabling treats another person as if they lack agency and ability.

Be proactive.

"An ounce of prevention is worth a pound of cure" is good medicine for parenting ails. Communicate expectations ahead of time. As much as possible, live prepared, not panicked.

Value interdependence over independence.

The height of maturity isn't independence; it's accepting our interdependent design. Much trouble in marriage and other relationships results from focusing on independence as the end goal of adolescence.

If they can't handle a "no," they're not ready for a "yes."

Prioritize fun.

Fun isn't a privilege to be earned. It is a necessity to endure and rise above life's difficulties.

Embrace "why."

Rather than perceiving "why" as a threat to your authority, seize it as an opportunity to teach life principles -- even if that's not their motivation in asking. Once you explain, if the "Why" gets turned into a "whine" or an interrogation, that's when you call "Game over."

Take your time.

When something catches you off guard, which it will, do not feel you have to respond or make a decision immediately. Buy yourself some time. Even if this isn't your regular habit, announce you're starting a practice of allowing sufficient time between being aware of a situation and deciding your response to it. You'll make better decisions and model a critical life skill.

Count the cost.

What people don't learn during childhood and adolescence, life will try to teach them as an adult -- and almost always at a much higher cost!

Celebrate!

What gets celebrated gets repeated. Recognize achievements -- whether behavioral, academic, relational, financial, or spiritual -- and be intentional to celebrate. This might be as simple as fixing a favorite meal or as grand as booking a cruise. It's not about expense; it's about recognition and affirmation!

Bonus Resources

It's risky recommending sources. I don't endorse or agree with 100% of anyone's views except mine. Even that's been known to change! There's always the possibility a year from now it will come out someone whose work I've recommended is living under an assumed identity and is on the FBI's most wanted list. Then I'll have to remove my recommendation and send an email to past buyers, "I didn't know anything about this!"

I didn't say this was probable; just possible. However, I still believe the reward for you outweighs the risks for me. That's the relationships between good authors and readers. (See what I did there? Risk, reward, relationship.) Read and listen for yourself. Discard what doesn't help and keep what does. And if you do discover someone whose work I've recommended is a secret spy, by all means, let me know -- after you notify the FBI.

Axis
Tons of resources including a newsletter, "The Culture Translator," which keeps you up to date with current events, trends, and pop culture adolescents are interested in or impacted by.
https://axis.org/

Fuller Youth Institute
Ample resources for parents, church, and youth leaders including books, blogs, and a podcast.
https://fulleryouthinstitute.org/

Growing Leaders

Although primarily geared to schools, there's valuable resources you can use personally or recommend to your school leaders. https://growingleaders.com/

Dr. Kevin Leman

Books, podcast, speaking engagements
Podcast, YouTube channel, blog, and other resources
https://birthorderguy.com/

Raising Boys & Girls

https://www.raisingboysandgirls.com/
Podcast, books, blog, conferences, and more

The Jury's Still Out

Enough research is showing major cultural shifts for adolescents, and we still don't know the long-term impact. For example, fewer adolescents are holding jobs during high school or even getting their driver's license. Many spend more time in the virtual world than the physical one.

These findings don't negate the importance of understanding the adolescent brain remodel. Rather, the significance is increased! As you read, ask yourself, what might the outcomes be when young people aren't engaging with peers and in activities as they've done in previous generations? Assuming it all turns out the same in the end is something we -- and our youth -- can't afford.

The Chicken or the Egg?

As young people are delaying many of the traditional activities of adulthood, such as marriage, living independently, and having children, researchers question how this is impacting the remodeling process of the adolescent brain. Is the brain's remodel taking longer than it did in the past because of these delays? Or was the process always the same?

It's impossible to know for certain, given the inability to travel back in time with today's technology. We know the brain affects actions and actions affect the brain. This reinforces a key concept throughout this book: Adolescence is a normal life stage, not an excuse to indulge in immaturity.

A Special Note for Educators

Teaching adolescents can be like winning a drawing for a Mediterranean cruise or being chosen as the next IRS auditee. Sometimes your experiences bounce between these two extremes in a single day!

Yet teachers can have profound impact on students, both positively and negatively. How many stories have we heard about how one teacher, coach, or mentor redirected a child's life? Sometimes this happens over a sustained period, and sometimes it's one interaction.

That's why I'm excited you're reading this book! While it won't offer a cure for all of what ails your students or school system, it can empower you with greater confidence, effectiveness, and empathy. You know the power of knowledge, and shared knowledge exponentially multiplies impact!

Advocate for this book to be required or highly recommended reading for your parents and staff. Meet with other readers to discuss how to apply the material inside and outside of the classroom. With parental and administrative approval, have students read and discuss this book. Adolescents love learning about themselves, and understanding the brain remodel process can powerfully influence their perspective, priorities, and decisions.

Be encouraged, my friend! For you truly have an impact that is immeasurable, eternal, and irreplaceable!

Science: Cement or Gelatin?

Very little categorized as "science" is truly unchangeable. The rotation of the earth, gravity, and cheesecakes that crack because a butterfly flaps its wings half a continent away are a few that we can count on. This book is based on in-depth research from several sources and perspectives. Therefore, the science reported is only as good as the science conducted.

No doubt there will be new findings in the years ahead which may alter some of the details. But the essentials of the brain's massive physiological remodel is established. I've avoided outliers and taken a conservative approach where data varies widely. This isn't "woo-woo" information. It's credible, transformative, and I hope to help make it common knowledge.

For Further Reading

The ideas, conclusions, and application suggestions in the following materials are not 100% approved by me. There are significant differences in consequential areas, including in foundational Christian beliefs. Pick the fruit; ignore the thorns.

iGen: Why Today's Super-Connected Kids Are Growing Up Less Rebellious, More Tolerant, Less Happy--and Completely Unprepared for Adulthood--and What That Means for the Rest of Us
Jean Twenge, Ph.D. ©2017, Simon & Schuster, Inc.

Grit: The Power of Passion and Perseverance
Angela Duckworth, ©2016, Scribner, An Imprint of Simon & Schuster, Inc.

Age of Opportunity: Lessons from the New Science of Adolescence
Laurence Steinberg, Ph.D. ©2014, Houghton Mifflin Harcourt

Brainstorm: The Power and Purpose of the Teenage Brain
Daniel J. Siegel, M.D. ©2013, Penguin Group

Made to Stick: Why Some Ideas Survive and Others Die
Chip Heath & Dan Heath, ©2007, 2008, Random House

How We Learn: The Surprising Truth About When, Where, and Why It Happens
Benedict Carey, ©2014, Random House

The Teenage Brain: A Neuroscientist's Survival Guide to Raising Adolescents and Young Adults
Frances E. Jensen with Amy Ellis Nutt, ©2015, Harper Collins

Born to Be Wild: Why Teens Take Risks, and How We Can Help Keep Them Safe
Jess P. Shatkin, M.D., Ph.D., ©2017 Penguin Random House

The Anxious Generation: How the Great Rewiring of Childhood is Causing an Epidemic of Mental Illness
Jonathan Haidt ©2024 Penguin Press

Empower Others

People with a shared vision and understanding give themselves and each other the gifts of strength and solutions. Invite others to buy this book and discuss it. Maybe use it to launch a parenting book club!

Having others who understand the great brain remodel of adolescence opens tremendous opportunities.

Together, you can:
- brainstorm creative solutions to problems;
- adopt practices, guidelines, and rules that others in your child's sphere will reinforce;
- influence policies in your child's education and activity programs;
- practice empathy and be mindful when you might be sliding into indulgence; and
- encourage each other to do the right thing when it's not the easy thing!

Adolescence doesn't have to be terrifying! Empower yourself and others to be confident, effective, and empathetic through this book!

Stay Connected

I'd love to hear from you!

Share your questions and insights via email at
stephanie@stephaniepresents.com
or through the contact form on the website:
https://www.stephaniepresents.com

Book me to speak at your church, school, home-school group, or faith-friendly organization.

Get Hi(Impact), a newsletter helping you multiply your impact at
https://www.stephaniepresents.com

For more print and digital resources, visit
https://www.key3press.com

Join the mission of building
spiritually strong,
emotionally healthy, and
relationally smart generations!